LOST
WIRRAL

LES JONES

AMBERLEY

For Andrew, Christopher and Daniel

First published 2019

Amberley Publishing
The Hill, Stroud
Gloucestershire, GL5 4EP

www.amberley-books.com

British Library Cataloguing in Publication Data.

A catalogue record for this book is available from the British Library.

ISBN 978 1 4456 9153 4 (print)
ISBN 978 1 4456 9154 1 (ebook)

Origination by Amberley Publishing.
Printed in the UK.

Contents

Have fun in sunny Cheshire !

New Brighton
WALLASEY

HOLIDAY GUIDE FROM PUBLICITY
MANAGER TOWN HALL WALLASEY

BRITISH RAILWAYS

TRAIN SERVICES AND FARES FROM
STATIONS OFFICES AND AGENCIES

Introduction

Two arrow falls from Chester city walls.

Domesday Book (1086)

The Wirral Peninsula is one of the most beautiful and diverse regions in Britain. Bounded to the north by the Irish Sea, to the west by the Dee and to the east by the Mersey, it is these two rivers that largely define its character. The western side facing the wide expanse of the slow-moving Dee retains its rural outlook, whereas the eastern side facing the fast-flowing and deeper River Mersey has become industrialised and urban.

This book seeks to highlight some of the many losses that have taken place on Wirral over the last 100 years, not only to the built environment but to a more sedate and peaceful way of life. The most palpable losses are to our streets and buildings, predominantly but not exclusively in the larger towns of Wallasey and Birkenhead, and these are discussed in the first two chapters. The loss of streetscapes has been caused by a variety of factors, including road widening for trams and buses, then latterly through the expansion of infrastructure to cope with the rise in car ownership. Many areas of Wirral were destroyed by the Luftwaffe during the Second World War, but the destruction was sustained by a coterie of insensitive planners and architects after the

Hoylake Road looking towards Moreton Cross, *c.* 1948.

Poole Road, Egremont, *c.* 1900.

war when more fine buildings were replaced by brutalist monstrosities. Although there have been some losses in the west of the peninsula, the major loss here has been to the green spaces between villages due to the relentless expansion of housing.

The pursuit of leisure has always been a contributory factor to the character of the peninsula, with West Kirby and Hoylake catering for the more discerning traveller while the loud and bawdy New Brighton provided the sort of entertainment day trippers from Liverpool and beyond desired. Much of the infrastructure of the leisure industry has been lost over the decades, with every one of the open-air pools torn down and the majority of cinemas and theatres closing. Wirral now has only one League football club with New Brighton FC's ground now given over to housing. All these losses and more are covered in section 3 of the book.

Section 4 covers the world of work and the losses caused by the rapid and ongoing changes in technology, from blacksmiths and glaziers to boatbuilders and quarrymen. All these skills have been lost or diminished over the last century with the adoption of advanced technologies. Retailers, whether in small outlets or in large department stores, have seen a massive change over the last decade due to the online revolution, and this trend is set to continue, with the consequential loss of individual shops and the overall vitality of many high streets. The advance of technology has affected workers in most fields of endeavour and the public sector is no exception; the work of our police and firemen is also examined in this section.

Any nostalgic look back at what we have lost over the years must include the evolution of public transport. Probably the greatest changes have been wrought on road transport and all aspects are illustrated here, from horse-drawn and electrified trams, diesel buses, and eventually back to trams in some parts of Birkenhead. The advent of the railways in the Victorian era opened up the peninsula for both trade and tourism and this mode of transport soon linked up with regular bus routes and ferries on the Mersey. One form of transport that did not quite catch on was the hovercraft, with

New Chester Road, Rock Ferry, *c.* 1902.

the first regular route in the United Kingdom being from Leasowe shore to Rhyl in the 1960s. All of these modes are covered in section 5.

Most of us remember our school days, either with a rosy glow of nostalgia tinged with sadness for our lost youth and friends half-forgotten, or as an interminable battle to get through the academic day, longing for the final bell and home time. Whether they were spent in a draughty old Victorian edifice or a smart new building, some of the many losses are detailed in the final chapter. The Education Act of 1870 made schooling compulsory for all five to twelve year olds and many of our larger schools were built at this time. Some have been demolished for housing, but some have been found imaginative communal uses. In the same way while many smaller primary schools have also been lost due to demographical changes, others have been found alternative functions, which is also discussed in section 6.

The Victorians did not create buildings for their functionality alone; they realised that they should be a visual asset in the environment, something on a human scale that had a sense of place and a capacity to uplift the soul. This philosophy has been dolefully lacking since the 1960s when architects in conjunction with like-minded planners decided to rip the heart out of neighbourhoods with mass clearances, replacing many beautiful buildings with dystopian piles of brutalist structures to further their modernist agendas. While many lessons have been learnt and a more reasoned approach to development now seems to prevail, vigilance is always required as bad architecture continues to blight our unique peninsula.

Exponential changes have occurred through advances in technology and are set to continue. While many benefits accrue from these changes, we should all take time out from our busy lives to appreciate what we already have. As this book illustrates in a small way, we have lost many fine buildings and streets and much social cohesion in the name of progress; perhaps we should rest awhile to appreciate and treasure what remains. As William Henry Davies famously said, 'What is this life if, full of care, we have not time to stand and stare.'

I

Lost Streets

Folly Lane, Wallasey Village, 1904.

This area of Wallasey Village has suffered more than any other part of the borough due to road widening, primarily to provide easier access to the expanding tram network. Every property in the view above was swept away to improve access from St Hilary Brow to Leasowe Road. Flats now occupy a site behind the row of old cottages shown on the left, while the site of the right-hand properties is now in the centre of the road.

Looking south towards Leasowe Road, the Travellers Rest public house is shown on this view from the early 1920s when H. H. Shaw was the licensee. The shops in the distance were once owned by the Abbott brothers, the nearest being a butcher's shop run by Henry while his brother Thomas ran a plastering business next door. These properties also fell victim to road widening in the early 1950s.

GROVE ROAD, WALLASEY.   "The Unique Series".

This view of Grove Road in Wallasey Village shows the semi-rural nature of much of Wallasey before the expansion of the tramways. The small building to the left was known as Summer Cottage. It was occupied in 1898 when this postcard was produced by Thomas Suckley who was the steward for nearby Wallasey Golf Club. This is where Dr Frank Stableford conceived the golf scoring system that bears his name in 1931. The taller house behind survives but the trees have gone.

Wallasey Village.

The photographer has positioned himself in the centre of Wallasey Village looking towards Harrison Drive in this delightful Edwardian scene, which is completely unrecognisable today. Most of the houses on either side of the road would have been rented by market gardeners who worked the fertile land to the north of Leasowe Road, an activity that continues to this day. The property jutting out at the end of the road is the Travellers Rest. All this side is now taken by St Mary's College.

The gentleman to the left in this view is walking towards Birkenhead Road in Seacombe from Dock Road, with Kelvin Road off to his left beyond the pillar box. Two of the shops behind him catered for the large number of hungry dockers from the nearby Great Float. Their thirst was also slaked by a wealth of nearby pubs including The Swan (latterly the Blazing Stump), The Mona Castle, The Great Float and The Bee Hotel.

Brighton Street in Seacombe is seen here decked out for the visit of George V and Queen Mary on 25 March 1914. The row of shops to the left lie between Brougham Road and Kenilworth Road and are the only surviving properties, the buildings to the right were demolished when the new Town Hall was built. The tram in the distance bound for Seacombe Ferry on Route S has just passed the Wesleyan Methodist Church, its spire just visible to the left.

Brighton Street was built up in the late 1800s, linking Seacombe directly to the expanding New Brighton. Sadly, practically all the properties shown in the Victorian view above have been demolished, the only survivor being the building in the distance with the pyramidal roof, which was the Five Bar Rest public house, now a social club. Little Street and Chapel Street lay to the left behind the low run of shops. The more substantial block to the right included Buchanans the greengrocers.

Marked as Victoria Road on this postcard view from 1900, the road's name was changed following a request by the Wallasey Fire Brigade, to avoid confusion with Victoria Road in New Brighton, becoming Borough Road. Lost properties shown here include William Gees Herbalist shop and Bernard Gray's boot repairers on the left, with Millers Tobacconists, the Stanley Arms Hotel and Moses Batemans toy shop to the right. The Irving Theatre is the tall building at the top of the road.

The solid-looking houses on Seacombe Promenade illustrated in these two postcards must have had an excellent view out across the River Mersey at a time when the river was teeming with shipping of all shapes and sizes. The land these houses stood on is now taken up by part of the ventilation system for the Kingsway road tunnel, built in 1971. Much admired by lovers of brutalist architecture, these huge concrete structures have been likened to a giant speaker system.

E. J. Moorhouse, the prolific local photographer responsible for the production of both of these rare cards, has turned his camera to face the Ferry Terminal in this view. The old Ferry clock tower can be seen in the left distance with part of the tall building being taken by the Seacombe Ferry Hotel, which catered mainly for travellers to Liverpool and beyond. Tudor Avenue is the road to the right, only the top section of which has been retained.

Church Street, Egremont

These large Victorian properties graced Church Street in Egremont for over seventy years until March 1941 when in three terrible days of destruction all the houses captured on this postcard were reduced to rubble by the Luftwaffe. The area was redeveloped after the war, mainly with low-rise maisonettes, but a high-rise block called Charter House was also built to a height of 107 feet. The single tramline pictured was part of a one-way system, Seacombe-bound trams went down Church Street while outward-bound trams went up Falkland Road.

Brighton Street, Seacombe

This unusual high-level view of Brighton Street was one of a series of hand-tinted postcards issued by John Valentine of Dundee during the Edwardian era. The road off to the left is Kenilworth Road, with the Wesleyan church on the corner of Rappart Road. An early motor car makes an appearance to the bottom left, rather lost in this scene but soon to be the catalyst for untold destruction in the name of progress.

King Street in Egremont has always been a major thoroughfare in the town and as a consequence did not suffer as many losses due to road widening. Caught in this view, however, is the magnificent portico of the Presbyterian Church, which served the area's spiritual needs until 1908 when the congregation moved to smaller premises. The building became the Lyceum cinema but burnt down in 1930. The Gaumont Palace cinema took its place and this is the building most remembered by old Wallaseyans.

This Edwardian postcard of Victoria Road in New Brighton captures the view between Waterloo Road and Windsor Street. All the buildings to the right have been demolished except for a block adjacent to Grosvenor Road. Towards the river the road has become unrecognisable as town houses and a new road layout have removed many of the reminders of when New Brighton was a seaside resort capable of rivalling Blackpool.

There have been many losses in Birkenhead over the years, with the two cards produced here showing the changes to the main shopping area of Grange Road. The top view shows the top of the road where the roundabout has been removed and the Grange Hotel pulled down to accommodate a branch of McDonald's. A large Asda store now looms behind the buildings to the left.

The only recognisable buildings in this radically changed view from the 1960s are the corner of Beatties (now House of Fraser) with the Hillman Imp and Sunbeam cars outside, the low wall of St Werburgh's Church to the left, and the tall former Co-op building in the distance. Everything else was lost when Birkenhead Shopping Precinct was created in the 1970s. The Ford Anglia is parked outside a branch of Décor, a once-popular DIY store.

This view was taken in 1937 and shows Grange Road in Birkenhead looking up towards Charing Cross with Beverleys store on the corner of Catherine Street. The tall building on the right was Robbs Department Store, which survived the destruction wrought on this part of the road when the giant Asda store was erected. The left side fared better with several of the buildings extant. Pykes the jewellers had premises here for many years.

Looking east towards Argyle Street, this postcard was taken in 1953 when the coronation celebrations for Elizabeth II were in full swing. These properties were all lost to the new shopping precinct, including Bentleys pawnbrokers, the Atlas Hotel next door, and Woodsons the grocers whose premises stood at the corner of Milton Street. Other streets lost at the same time included Pym Street, Collingwood Street and Huskisson Street, which had St John's Church on an island site in its centre.

The Chester Arms is captured here in a view of Hamilton Street in the 1950s before all the property shown was demolished in the 1970s. It was lucky to survive into the twentieth century, however, as major damage was done to the building when tunnelling for the Mersey Railway undermined the foundations of the pub in 1885. The only buildings remaining are the hydraulic tower of Hamilton Square station and the Town Hall in the distance; the tall ventilation chimney did not survive.

The road to the near left in this view led up to a pub called the Happy Valley, so named because Borough Road follows the route of an old tributary of the River Mersey – hence its circuitous route and the fact that all roads off to the north and south lead down to it. All the property shown here has been lost other than No. 375 to the right, which still stands on the corner of Willmer Road.

The Promenade, looking South, Hoylake

Posted in September 1905, this postcard shows North Parade in Hoylake with Edwardian ladies enjoying a stroll in the summer sunshine. The property to the left has survived but the lighthouse in the middle distance has not been so lucky. Known as the lower light, it was used in conjunction with the upper light in Valentia Road, which still exists as a private house to aid navigation into the Hoyle Bank by mariners entering the Mersey.

Punch Bowl, Hoylake

This view of Hoylake is from around the same time and shows the second incarnation of the Punch Bowl public house in Market Street. The first pub sited here was a smaller affair with a picturesque thatched roof. The one shown here survived until 1936 even though it had always caused a bottleneck due to its awkward angle to the road. The current pub closed in 2014 with part of the building now taken by a plumber's merchants.

Moreton Cross has changed radically since this postcard view was taken in the 1920s. The low wall in the centre enclosed a small grassed area called the Plantation, which was lost when the odd-shaped roundabout was put in place. The white building to the right is the original Coach and Horses public house, which was demolished when the much larger pub was built behind, the original pub site now being part of the service road.

This 1960s view of Moreton shows Pasture Road (originally Station Road) looking towards the shore. The Tesco store was one of the earliest on Wirral, and a little further towards The Cross is a branch of Heavyseges, which were a locally based off-licence chain. The black-and-white building was once the Moreton Picture House and opened in 1921, playing silent movies until 1930. It closed in 1964 and somewhat predictably became a bingo hall.

This rare view of Moreton Cross captures a time before the kidney-shaped roundabout was introduced. Famous local jockey Francis 'Titch' Mason built the row of houses on the right, which still bear the names of many of his winning horses, including Kirkland, which he rode to victory in the Grand National in 1905. He was so gifted that he was paid £300 *not* to ride for a fortnight before the big race to avoid injury!

This view shows Moreton Cross some thirty years later with the large Plough Inn to the right, which replaced an earlier, smaller pub in 1931. This in turn was demolished, with a Tesco Express taking the site. Local branches of banks have fared as badly as pubs in recent years with the Lloyds bank to the left now operating as an Italian restaurant, which has also expanded into the tobacconist-cum-hairdresser next door.

LANE IN PRENTON.

"The Unique Series".

This view of a lane in Prenton dates from 1910 and shows the rural nature of this part of Birkenhead. This pastoral scene was to remain unchanged for most of the twentieth century until the land was built on in the 1950s. A small fragment has, however, endured in the area around Roman Road, near to another remarkable survivor, Prenton Hall, an old sandstone farmhouse that is now surrounded by modern housing.

UPTON, NEAR BIRKENHEAD.

THE UNIQUE SERIES.

This postcard of Upton village was taken around the same time as the view above as part of the Unique Series of cards. It shows the view from the crossroads towards St Mary's Church. Losses here include the fine Doric porch of the Eagle and Crown pub and the grand Georgian house behind the wall. The farm buildings to the left have been replaced by a pair of modern shops.

Most of the major changes to the streetscape of Wirral have occurred in Birkenhead and Wallasey, but the smaller towns and villages have not completely escaped the march of 'progress'. This postcard captures the view north towards High Street in Neston with the former White Horse pub on the left. Many public houses have closed in the area, which once boasted several breweries noted for the quality of their beer. The Brown Horse opposite still trades, however.

Looking back towards the Cross, the photographer has captured another lost pub. The large building to the right was the Golden Lion, which was replaced by a characterless shop in the 1950s. Much of Neston High Street has been damaged by unsympathetic infill but luckily the Town Hall remains, although shorn of its ornate railings, which were removed for the war effort and never replaced.

West Kirby is really two towns in one: the newer parts to the north-west catered for day trippers to the beach who arrived in their thousands by train. The old village remained an untouched enclave until relatively recently. This postcard captures a rather more tranquil way of life in Village Road at the turn of the last century. The shops have departed and the cottages reordered, but the lane remains as narrow as ever.

Similarly, Heswall is divided into two distinct areas, Lower and Upper, the former being the quieter residential part. The view here is of Village Road looking north, showing the village shop, which still serves the area today, although the furthest gable has been demolished and its fine Hovis sign has unfortunately disappeared. The sandstone building on the right housed the post office for many years but is now used as a hairdressers.

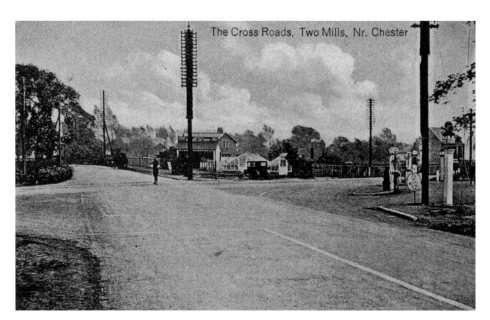

The Cross Roads, Two Mills, Nr. Chester

This rare view shows what is now a very busy crossroads at Two Mills in rather more tranquil times. The traffic policeman is standing where the Welsh Road and the Top Chester Road (A540) converge – not an advisable spot to linger today. Petrol pumps have just made an appearance to the right and the area behind the policeman would soon become home to the Eureka Café, a famous meeting point for cycling enthusiasts.

PRENTON HILL, BIRKENHEAD.

Much admired by Nikolaus Pevsner, the world-renowned architectural historian, Prenton Hill is a first-class Edwardian suburb created among existing pine woods. Businessmen from Liverpool made their homes in this area to take advantage of the stunning views back towards Liverpool and over the Wirral Peninsula to the distant Welsh hills. Many of these mansions have been lost and there has been some unsympathetic infill that jars the eye, but there is still much to enjoy here.

IRBY VILLAGE.

This evocative streetscape is from a postcard of 1902 and shows the view down Thingwall Road in Irby village towards its junction with Irby Road. The thatched cottage on the near right was the only shop in the village at this time. The large white building with its gable end to the road was Rookery Cottage. The rural character was sadly lost when all these properties were demolished, and utilitarian shops built in their place.

Barnston Village.

This Unique Series postcard is of a similar date and shows Barnston Road heading towards the recently refurbished Fox and Hounds pub, near to its junction with Storeton Road, one of the most awkward junctions in Wirral due to the lack of road widening. This is the former site of Barnston village school, known as Beechfield, which was opened in 1852 as a replacement for one in Woodchurch, some 3 miles away. Unlike Irby, Barnston has managed to retain much of its rural identity.

All the properties shown on this stretch of Upper Mersey Street in Ellesmere Port have been completely destroyed and today the road runs through an underpass below the roaring traffic of the M53. It is now the western route into the Ellesmere Port Boat Museum, but at one time it housed many of the men who worked in the port when it was a busy transhipment point for the Shropshire Union and Manchester Ship Canals.

The photographer of this Edwardian postcard has captured the view down Village Road in Higher Bebington at a time when the road was still semi-rural. The right side of the road past the railings was yet to be built up and the properties in Mersey View to the left were still operating as retail premises, but like so many shops in Wirral they have now been converted to domestic use.

2

Lost Buildings

Birkenhead YMCA, home of the Scout Movement and British basketball.

This single-storey, gabled building contained the living accommodation for the Halfpenny Bridge toll-keeper and was sited just beyond the current bridge over Wallasey Pool. Many older locals still call it the 'Penny Bridge', which it became known as when the toll was doubled. It was torn down soon after the toll was abolished. The area beyond the tollhouse was later developed as a coal dock, but this has subsequently been filled in – some rails being the only reminder of its existence.

This postcard, posted to Birkenhead in 1906, shows one of the many thatched cottages lost to redevelopment in the twentieth century. This example was pulled down in the 1930s when the site was cleared for Hebron Hall on the corner of Egerton Grove and Liscard Village. The two-storey property to the left is now the site of Manor Health Centre. Cottages such as these give an idea of the rural nature of most of Wallasey at this time.

Brighton Street, Seacombe

All the property to the left in this view of Brighton Street looking towards Seacombe was lost when the new Town Hall was constructed in the 1910s. Although the public house on the right survives it is no longer open, such has been the fate of so many pubs in the last ten years. Lost pubs nearby include The Bird In Hand, The Kings Arms, The Prince Albert, The Shepherds Rest and the Marine Hotel.

Mariners' Home from Promenade, Egremont

The loss of this notable landmark was greatly mourned by the people of Wallasey when it was pulled down in 1981. Land was given by Roger Jones, a Liverpool merchant, to provide accommodation for aged mariners. The main block shown in the postcard above was paid for by William Cliff in remembrance of his daughter and became known as Cliff House. It housed sixty-five single men and was finished in 1880. Married men were catered for in smaller cottages within the grounds.

This long-lost villa was located at the western end of Greenheys Road in Liscard, its old wall and gateway surviving until the recent development of new hospital facilities obliterated all traces of its existence. Built in the 1850s, its name was Highfield and after being purchased by the Corporation it became the first maternity hospital in Wallasey. After its almost total destruction in an air raid, maternity services were moved into Mill Lane Hospital, the department retaining the name of the old house.

Liscard Hall was built around 1835 for Sir John Tobin, merchant and former mayor of Liverpool. It was eventually sold to Wallasey Corporation who opened up the grounds as Central Park, which remains an important amenity in the town. After serving as the School of Art for many years the hall became vacant and therefore a target for vandals who managed to burn it to the ground in 2008 – yet another grievous loss to our architectural heritage.

This rare postcard shows the view west along Wallasey Road at the turn of the last century. The original Wellington Hotel is to the right and a once common thatched cottage is next door. A sign for Pritchards fruiterers can just be made out further down. Members of this family ran a house removals firm in the town for many years with premises where Wilko's store stands today. The properties beyond the hotel were lost when Coronation Buildings were constructed in 1937.

In the 1970s there were still over sixty public houses in Wallasey. The total is now less than half of this figure as social patterns change and more people consume alcohol at home. The pub shown on this card was the Primrose Hotel, which was demolished in 1923. A larger pub was built on the site and is still currently trading. The name is derived from a paddle steamer that plied the Mersey between Liverpool and Seacombe.

This fine painting by noted local artist Harry Hopps is of Poulton Hall in Wallasey around 1890 when it was occupied by Alfred Chantrell Hopps, Harry's uncle. Other noted owners were William Smith and David Buchanan, both cotton merchants from Liverpool. The property stood at the corner of Mill Lane and Poulton Road near where Poulton Hall Road now stands, having been demolished in 1933.

Now trading as a shoe shop, this building was once the Liscard Electric Palace, the second purpose-built cinema in Wallasey, which opened in 1911. It is hard to imagine today but the front was once an architectural extravaganza of baroque exuberance, made even more spectacular at night when it was illuminated by hundreds of lights. Showing silent films originally, The Palace witnessed the dawn of 'talkies' and colour before its popularity waned, closing its doors in 1959 – one of three Wallasey cinemas to close that year.

The foundation stone for Victoria Central Hospital was laid in 1889 and the hospital went on to serve the people of Wallasey for over ninety years before it was demolished in 1982 when Arrowe Park Hospital opened. Some of its functions (and its name) were moved to the old Isolation Hospital site in Mill Lane and an ambulance station was built on part of the cleared site. The A&E department later became St George's Residential and Nursing Home.

This grand building was originally a convalescent home for women and girls. It was located in the lower half of Rowson Street in New Brighton, where Nelson Court flats now stand. Built in 1847, it contained seventy-four beds where female patients could recover from illness in the breezy seaside air. Male patients were admitted during the First World War to aid recuperation. It is better remembered by locals, however, as the Maris Stella Convent, which it became in 1945, closing its doors in 1965.

Whetstone Lane Fire Station in Birkenhead is captured in this postcard from 1905. Opened ten years earlier to replace a smaller facility in Tranmere, it had a staff of fourteen firemen and was operational until replaced by a new station in 1973, sited in nearby Exmouth Street. The Birkenhead Fire Brigade was administered for many years by Chief Fire Officer Burns. The site was eventually taken by a branch of budget supermarket Netto.

192   CENTRAL LIBRARY, BIRKENHEAD.

Andrew Carnegie was a Scottish-born American steel magnate and philanthropist who used much of his fortune to establish libraries in over 400 British towns and cities. The Birkenhead Carnegie Library, built in 1909, was situated in Market Street, lasting a mere twenty-five years before it was demolished to make way for the approaches to the Mersey Road Tunnel. A new library was built half a mile away in Borough Road, which was opened in 1934 by George V.

Captured on this postcard from 1908 is the premises of the North End Liberal Club on the corner of St Anne's Street and Duke Street in Birkenhead. Although the building survives, it is completely derelict and looks in danger of falling into the street. The building jutting out further down was St Anne's School, which has since been demolished. St Anne's Street was once one of the longest in the gridiron layout, but this section is now a mere cul-de-sac.

This sunny view from the 1920s shows the lower end of Grange Mount, with Grange Road West beyond. Behind the wall to the left stood Birkenhead Lying-In (Maternity) Hospital, housed in an imposing Georgian-style building of 1846. Known locally as 'Grange Mount', it is where thousands of Birkonians were born and holds fond memories for many. It was closed after obstetric services were centralised at Arrowe Park but not demolished until 2001, with Thomas Court flats eventually taking the site.

Now a furniture store, this building was once the Gaumont Cinema, Birkenhead. Constructed in 1937 in a pale art deco style, it provided accommodation for no fewer than 1,700 customers, which gives a fair idea of the popularity of the film business in the 1930s. Like all cinemas in the 1960s, the Gaumont suffered falling attendances due to competition from television and closed in 1964, with the last film being *Journey to the Centre of the Earth*. Its subsequent uses have included bingo, snooker and even an ice rink.

Another large cinema to open in the 1930s was the Plaza in Borough Road, Birkenhead. As with most of the grander cinemas, customers were enticed in by the magnificent décor. The Plaza boasted a walnut-panelled vestibule and mohair drapes across the massive screen; it also, unfortunately, had an asbestos safety screen. Its demise had a familiar ring about it: falling attendances, a change of use to bingo and the end for yet another cinema in a town that once, at its apogee, boasted twenty.

Vast swathes of terraced housing were destroyed in the 1970s and 1980s in downtown Birkenhead to make way for Europa Boulevard, Conway Park station and Europa Pools Leisure Centre. One of the best remembered properties lost during this time was The Angel Inn, which stood on the corner of Beckwith Street and Camden Street, a thoroughfare that no longer exists but originally ran from Conway Street to Brook Street. The site of the pub is now taken by the new station.

During demolition The Angel stood in splendid isolation for a number of years. Pubs were usually the last properties to be pulled down as the licence to sell alcohol was extremely prized and not given up lightly. Older Birkonians will remember many of the lost streets in this area, including Erskine Street, Rhyl Street, Kinmel Street and Clwyd Street. The Angel was one of the earliest pubs in the so-called gridiron. The only notable survivor is the Queens Hotel in Park Road East.

Nearly all the small hospitals in Wirral were closed and subsequently pulled down when the 1,000-bed Arrowe Park Hospital opened in the mid-1980s. One of these casualties was the Birkenhead General Hospital which was located on Park Road North between Livingstone Street and Prince Edward Street. Opened in 1863 as the Borough Hospital, it served the town until 1982 when it was lost to vandalism and ultimate demolition.

Happily, some of the old hospital buildings did survive the wrecking ball and were put to other uses. The postcard above illustrates the former children's hospital in Woodchurch Road, Birkenhead, which survives as a residential care home. Many older Birkonians will remember Winston, the huge teddy bear in the waiting area that was earmarked for relocation to the Paediatric Department at Arrowe Park Hospital, but unfortunately turned to dust when an attempt was made to move it.

The reason many old pubs were named The Coach and Horses was often because the old stagecoach would stop at these inns to enable passengers to refresh themselves and horses to be changed. The former pub seen here would have been on a main route to the north of Wirral before the Top Chester Road was built. It dates from the late eighteenth century and remained in business until 2007 when it closed as a pub, reopening in 2013 as a Greek taverna.

Formerly known as The Vaults, then The Letters and finally as the Neston Hotel, this building dates from the 1870s and is pictured here in 1904 when Mr W. A. Higginbottom was the licensee. It remained open until the mid-1930s when it closed for good. It had a new, but brief, lease of life during the Second World War as the headquarters of the local ARP section but this was merely a stay of execution as the property was eventually demolished and houses built on the site.

One of the most grievous architectural losses to Wirral in the past 100 years has been the destruction of Dawpool, a large mansion that overlooked the Dee at Thurstaston. It was commissioned by Thomas Henry Ismay, owner of the White Star Shipping Line, and was built between 1882 and 1886. The architect was Richard Norman Shaw, who also designed New Scotland Yard on Victoria Embankment in London, and the White Star Headquarters in Liverpool, both of which still stand.

Ismay moved out in 1907, and after a stint as an orthopaedic hospital during the First World War, it was bought by Sir Henry Roberts, who to his eternal shame had it demolished in 1927. This act of utter philistinism robbed posterity of one of Shaw's greatest works, one of only three large houses he designed. Remnants of the house survive, including large fireplaces at the Kingsland in Borough Road, Birkenhead, and Clough Williams-Ellis' confection at Portmeirion in North Wales.

Hooton Hall.

Another fine house was lost when Hooton Hall was demolished in 1932. Built for Sir William Stanley by Samuel Wyatt in 1788 in the fashionable classical style, it remained in the family for just seventy years before being sold to a Liverpool banker to cover vast gambling debts. The new owner added a large orangery and the distinctive clock tower. After use as a military hospital in the First World War it was left empty and was finally pulled down, with Vauxhall Motors eventually taking the site.

Shakespeare Cottages, Poet's Corner, Port Sunlight.

The internationally renowned model village of Port Sunlight was the brainchild of William Lever, later Lord Leverhulme, and was inaugurated in 1888 with houses and social amenities added during the next twenty years. There have been few losses in the village, but one of the saddest was the demolition of Shakespeares Cottages on Poets Corner in 1938, captured here on a postcard issued by Levers themselves. Losses also occurred two years later when the Collegium and houses in Bolton Road were destroyed in air raids.

There has been a hall at Bromborough since 1100, in the form of a moated grange, but the Georgian-style hall illustrated here was put up in 1617. Situated to the east of the village, it was a fine location with views across the Mersey and beyond. Unfortunately, the site was in the way of a bypass to the A41 and this led to its demolition in 1932. The current Royal Oak pub occupies a position roughly where the hall stood.

Bebington Hall stood to the right-hand side of Civic Way and was needlessly demolished in 1965 to make way for an important grass verge. The hideous brutalist library building on the opposite side merely adds to the windswept emptiness of the site, standing in mute testament to the hubris and conceit of planners and architects of the time who seemed to know the cost of everything and the value of nothing.

3

Sports and Leisure

Ogden's cigarette card from their AFC Nicknames series.

Since its creation by James Atherton and William Rowson, the pre-eminent leisure centre on Wirral has been that of New Brighton. This wide view captures the old Palace Amusement Emporium to the right, a row of gabled shops catering for the thousands of day trippers in the centre, and a taller row known as the Ham and Egg Parade, which contained eating houses and bed and breakfast establishments, some of which had rather dubious reputations. Looming above it all was the popular but short-lived Tower.

The New Brighton Tower was 621 feet above sea level and was a major attraction in itself. The large red-brick building at its base also had its fair share of amusements, as this delightful postcard view illustrates. The ballroom was one of the largest in the world and incorporated a sprung floor and a special stage for dance bands. It famously hosted the Beatles on several occasions before its tragic demise in an all-consuming fire in 1969.

This view from the early 1900s shows the front at New Brighton by the bottom of Rowson Street before the large boating lake was constructed. In the foreground a pair of long-suffering donkeys struggle across the sand with a pair of overdressed ladies aboard, while others laze in the shade of cocoon-like baskets – a forerunner of the deckchair. Marine Promenade and Marine Lake were built here between 1906 and 1908 and proved very popular. It is now, however, a public order offence to jump into the lake – punishable by a £1,000 fine.

The original New Brighton pier was a rickety wooden affair built by William Rowson in 1830, rebuilt some thirty years later in iron. This version was replaced in 1931, but with falling visitor numbers after the war it fell into a slow and painful decline. The End of The Pier Show commenced in 1978. All that remained was this rather tawdry amusement centre called The Golden Goose, which was itself demolished in the 1980s.

There were no televisions, PlayStations or other distractions in 1910 when this view was taken. People made their own amusements by marching up the main street, in this case Wallasey Village, led by a smartly dressed silver band and followed by various floats. The occasion was the Wallasey Village Festival, which was held annually and included a Rose Queen and races in nearby Belvidere Field. The spire belonged to the United Reformed Church, which still stands; all the other property was cleared for road widening.

At first sight this scene appears to capture some innocent fun down on Wallasey Shore where sand modelling is taking place in this rare view of 1914. The sand sculpture to the left bears the legend 'His Last Farewell' and includes a soldier and his mount, referencing the onset of the First World War. Many of the male onlookers seen here would soon be heading for the trenches of Flanders, but how many would return?

Both of the group photographs on this page were taken by J. Wilkinson, a local photographer with a studio in Manville Road, New Brighton. This view of an open-air religious service was taken in July 1914 on the sands in front of Marine Park Mansions, which had recently been built on Wellington Road – one of the original thoroughfares in James Atherton's ambitious scheme to make New Brighton the greatest seaside resort in the North West.

Leisure activities of a different sort are captured here by Mr Wilkinson as members of North Wirral Tennis Club pose for the camera in Harrison Park in around 1920. The special occasion is not known, but it may have been a celebration for Lottie Dod, a world-champion tennis player from nearby Bebington who won the Ladies Singles at Wimbledon on five occasions. Tennis is still played in the park along with cricket and bowls.

One of the most grievous losses in the slow decline of New Brighton from the 1970s onwards were the baths – the largest open-air pool in the world when built in 1934. They played host to the Miss New Brighton competition for many years as well as pop concerts, *It's a Knockout* and fireworks displays. Following a storm in 1987 the fabric of the building was so badly damaged that the council were forced to demolish it, with Morrisons and a cinema eventually taking the site.

Entertainment on a smaller scale was provided further along New Brighton Promenade by a miniature boating lake adjacent to the pier. Overlooking the junior mariners stood The Tivoli Theatre, which hosted world-class entertainers such as Lily Langtry, the 'Jersey Lily'. It suffered the fate of many theatres and became an amusement arcade before being demolished in 1976 after a fire. The dark brown building at the foot of Victoria Road became the Chelsea Reach nightclub. All of this row is now residential.

Founded in 1921, New Brighton Football Club were members of the Football League from 1923 until 1951, spending twenty-one seasons in the old Division 3 North. This great action photograph is from the 1950s at the Tower Athletics Ground (New Brighton are in the white shirts) with the Tower Ballroom looming in the background. Although the capacity of the ground was a very impressive 80,000, The Rakers' record attendance was just 16,000.

With such a large stadium available it is no wonder that it was utilised for other sports, particularly in the popular summer season when it was used for running and cycling events, including the World Cycling Championships in 1922. The running track was removed and a speedway track put down in 1933, and later on it became a stock car racing circuit. The large area of land behind the stands was also put to good use as a parade ground for the local militia as seen in the very rare postcard above.

ARGYLE STREET, BIRKENHEAD. B.H.12

Probably the most famous theatre on Wirral was the Argyle in Birkenhead. Opened in December 1868 it contained not only a stage but five bowling alleys and a large billiards room. Its apogee was in the 1890s through to the 1920s when it became a music hall, playing host to such luminaries as Harry Lauder, Dan Leno, Charlie Chaplin and Stan Laurel. Its demise came suddenly in September 1940 when a German bomb scored a direct hit, causing a fire that led to the theatre's complete destruction.

CONWAY STREET, BIRKENHEAD. B.H.15.

Opening on 26 May 1917, the Empire Picture House is captured here to the right in Conway Street, Birkenhead, on this Feilden postcard from *c.* 1934. Originally showing silent films, it was the second cinema in Birkenhead to show talkies when in August 1929 it showed *The Doctors Secret*. A modernisation in the mid-1930s produced the ghastly frontage seen today. It soldiered on into the 1990s as a cinema before succumbing to the inevitable and closing its doors.

This fine edifice on the corner of Clarence Road and Borough Road was once the residence of Peter Rothwell, a prominent builder in Birkenhead around the turn of the last century. In later years it became the home of the Merseyside Bridge Centre, a widespread social activity that continues to grow in popularity throughout Wirral. Although the fine railings surrounding the property went for the war effort in 1940, the house is fortunately largely unchanged.

Bowling, whether flat green or crown green, retains its popularity today, but unfortunately many bowling greens have been lost to redevelopment. The group photograph shown here is of the Oddfellows Bowling Club who played in Central Park and also at Oxton Park Wallasey, one of the lost greens. The photograph was taken alongside the easternmost green in Central Park and shows the author's father and grandfather and fellow bowlers with a fine array of silverware.

You are now a WOLF CUB
I trust you to
DO YOUR BEST
Charles Maclean.
Chief Scout.

Wirral became the cradle of the Scout Movement when Lord Baden Powell inaugurated the Cub Scout Movement in Birkenhead in 1910. The oldest scout group in the world that is still active is the 2nd Birkenhead in North Road (the 1st Birkenhead based at the old YMCA has been disbanded), and the 3rd World Scout Jamboree was held in Arrowe Park in 1929. The wolf cub enrolment card shown here was issued to Alan Jones of the 18th Wallasey Group in 1962.

Raby Mere is a pleasant place to visit but has lost many of its attractions over the years. The original purpose of the mere was to drive a waterwheel for grinding corn but the potential to attract tourists to this beauty spot led to the introduction of rowing boats, swings and a very popular café. There was also a small collection of amusement machines including an 'electric shock' machine. All of these have gone but feeding the ducks remains a pleasant pastime, although even this is frowned upon in certain quarters.

Known locally just as The Hydro, the West Kirby Hydropathic Hotel was a landmark in the resort from its opening in 1896 through to its demolition in 1972. Advertised as the 'Sanitorium of the North', it boasted Turkish, Russian, vapour and electric baths, the last of which does sound a little troubling. Many famous guests stayed at the hotel to take advantage of the health-giving air and the fine views across to North Wales, including the Aston Villa football team in 1959.

The Royal Hotel in Hoylake was built by Lord Stanley in 1792. A fine Georgian building, 'handsome and commodious', as one guest asserted, it served as a base for numerous activities such as bathing, shooting, riding and walking. The spacious grounds eventually became the course for the world-famous Royal Liverpool Golf Club, but this did not save it from wanton destruction in 1958, a foretaste of the architecturally disastrous decades to follow.

Park.

Birkenhead.

In 1833 the Select Committee for Public Walks (for there was such a thing!) began to promote the provision of parks that they felt would promote a healthier use of Sundays. Music at the time was seen as a moral influence that occasioned the construction of bandstands in many Victorian parks, including the one illustrated above in Birkenhead Park overlooking the Lower Lake. Although the structure remains, it is currently not in use as a bandstand.

The fine ensemble above would doubtless have played in Birkenhead Park but there were others available at the time. Examples at Hoylake Promenade and Central Park in Wallasey have been lost, along with no fewer than three in New Brighton (Marine Park, Victoria Gardens and at the end of the pier), but Vale Park bandstand remains as a major asset to the town with shows performed throughout the summer.

No chapter on leisure would be complete without mention of dining out. This view from 1908 is taken from an advertising postcard for Banks & Cookes Crescent Café, which stood on the corner of Banks Road and The Crescent in West Kirby. It advertised 'Room to seat 500, picnic and school parties catered for'. Eating out was still a rare and special event up until the 1970s with the likes of Berni Inns offering prawn cocktails, steaks and Black Forest gateaux.

MT 6   MORETON COMMON

Cubs and scouts did not have a monopoly on camping in the last century, as this postcard of Moreton shore in the 1950s attests. Whole families would head to the coast and pitch up for the day, armed with sandwiches and bottles of pop or even sugared water if funds did not allow. Simple pleasures such as this seem to have been lost in the social miasma of Facebook and Twitter.

Two more valuable Wirral amenities were lost when Hoylake and West Kirby baths closed. Hoylake baths, illustrated here, were opened in 1913, but due to functional problems were completely rebuilt from 1928 in an art deco style, reopening in 1931. Some English Championship races were held here, and it had a brief stint as an ARP base in the war. It was demolished in the 1980s but some traces of it remain.

West Kirby Swimming Club formed in 1900 and utilised the boating lake for their activities for many years. A purpose-built swimming pool was built in a piecemeal fashion from 1913, with shelters constructed first followed by the concrete apron and changing rooms. The west side remained open to the river, however, which allowed jellyfish to enter the baths, causing the lifeguards to fish them out into wire baskets. A concrete island was also built with water chutes and slides. Traces of these baths also remain.

4

The World of Work

Tittley's Chandlery Store, Upton.

Cammell Lairds shipbuilders have been one of the major employers in Birkenhead for well over 100 years. William Laird founded an ironworks in 1824, which quickly expanded, necessitating a move to a larger site on the banks of the Mersey. His firm joined forces with steel producers Johnson Cammell in 1903 and they went on to produce some of the largest and most famous ships in the world. Unfortunately, the company has lost its pre-eminence in ship construction and repair, although it endures on a smaller scale.

The two images on this page were produced by Cammell Lairds as a set of postcards during the First World War and as they showed some of the industrial processes involved in ship-making they had to be passed for publication by the official censor. The top view shows one of the cavernous machine shops with the lower picture showing workers forging files in a sea of steam-driven belts. The skills involved in manual forging have now been mostly lost with the advent of power hammers.

This picturesque postcard of Parkgate fishermen on the middle slip was taken in the 1930s before the relentless advance of sparta grass had literally choked the life out of the industry. This grass had been deliberately planted on the North Wales side of the Dee to stabilise the mudflats, but had extended across the river to the Wirral side where it continues to spread to this day. Shrimps are still caught in certain areas of the estuary and sold in local shops on The Parade.

This historic photograph shows colliers ending their final shift at Neston Colliery in 1927. The area is now a peaceful haven for wildlife but in its heyday this area was the cradle of the Industrial Revolution on the peninsula. The first steam engines on Wirral were used to pump water out of the mine workings, which stretched far out below the Dee. At its height 300 people were employed at the mine working up to 100 hours per week, including children as young as nine.

Ardle & Sons were drum and keg makers from Wallasey, products used in the brewing and chemical industries. The decorated horse shown in this rare view would have been adorned in this manner to pull a float or wagon in a local festival, possibly the Central Park Fair or the May Queen celebrations. The wagon behind was owned by Arthur V. Crutchley, whose descendants continue to operate the firm today.

Basnetts were lead light makers around the turn of the last century with premises off Demesne Street in Seacombe. The making of lead lights involved joining small pieces of glass, often stained or coloured, into lead cames to make a complete window. This could range from small casement windows for domestic use, to large stained-glass windows for churches. The requirement for such expertise has been lost, with such work now undertaken by a select few specialists.

This fine band of constables in their shako hats are walking along Claremount Road in Wallasey on the occasion of Edward VII's coronation in 1911. They would have been members of the Cheshire Constabulary at this time as the Wallasey Borough Police were not formed until April 1913.The houses being built in the background were in the area of Sedburgh Road. The commandant of the special constabulary in Wallasey at one time was PC Crook.

Fast-forward to the 1970s where the police are attending an explosion at the Abbey Gas Company on the corner of Duke Street and Cleveland Street in Birkenhead. This part of the town was accustomed to explosions as the previous building was destroyed by bombing in the Second World War – a piece of shrapnel was placed on the rebuilt building as a reminder of the event. In the 1970s police patrol cars had a broad red stripe on them, so were known as 'Jam Butty' cars.

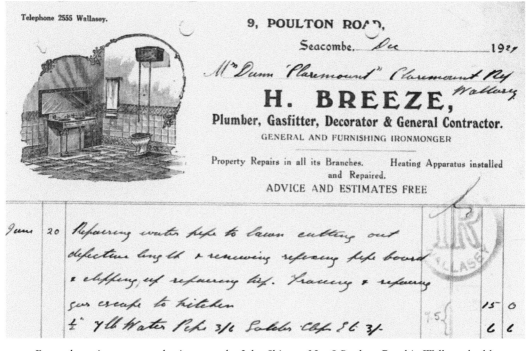

Formerly an ironmongery business run by John Skinner, No. 9 Poulton Road in Wallasey had become the workplace of H. Breeze's plumbing business in the 1920s, as this fine letterhead attests. He must have run a reasonably successful business as he had enough money to own his own telephone, still a rare asset in 1929. The fact that Mr Breezes client on this invoice lived at Claremount, a very large house in a salubrious part of town, may give a clue to his standard of work.

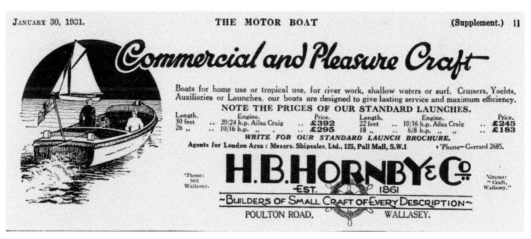

Cammell Lairds were not the only company designing and making boats in north Wirral in the 1930s, as this rare advertisement from *Motor Boat* magazine proves. H. B. Hornby & Co. were boatbuilders on a small scale in Wallasey, with premises in Gorsey Lane, near its junction with Gorsedale Road. A 30-foot launch cost £392 in 1931, the equivalent of just under £25,000 today, which was probably a bargain as a new Chapparal 29-foot speedboat would set you back nearly £100,000 today.

This magnificent-headed invoice is indicative of the intrinsic beauty of Edwardian printing; even the most mundane of products such as cigarette packets and soap powder boxes were given the most intricate designs, a truly golden but lost age when such things mattered. The Gandy Belt Company set up in Wheatland Lane Wallasey in 1852, making a variety of driving belts for machinery and latterly brake and clutch linings. The enterprise survived a devastating fire in 1927 but eventually closed the site in 1985, moving to Birkenhead.

MORETON VILLAGE, BIRKENHEAD.

Most parts of Wirral retain their rural identity to a greater or lesser extent, but at the beginning of the last century almost 80 per cent of workers were employed in agriculture. This fine scene of cows being driven up the main road in Moreton is from 1904 and illustrates just how much the character of some Wirral villages has changed. There are two pubs in this view: the sandstone pub on the right was the Plough Inn, which survived until 1937; the Coach and Horses in the distance lasted ten years less. Both were rebuilt as larger pubs.

The lack of any means of refrigeration during most of the last century meant that milk and other dairy products were produced locally. Small dairies such as this one, which stood in Breck Road, Wallasey, would deliver milk in horse-drawn carts to customers each day in large metal churns. Increases in population made these smaller outlets uneconomical, with larger dairies taking their place. Many Wirralians will remember the large dairy on Woodchurch Road – now a car showroom.

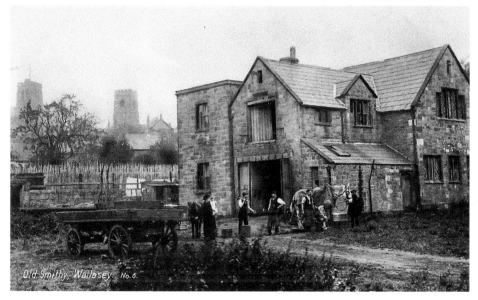

Before the advent of the internal combustion engine, most forms of work, especially those involving the movement of produce, was undertaken by horses. The local smithy therefore provided a vital service, keeping the equine population suitably shod. The one illustrated here was situated at the bottom end of School Lane in Wallasey Village. The building was originally the village infant school, but proved too small for this purpose. A builder purchased the property and subsequently leased it to the local blacksmith in 1915.

When William Hesketh Lever came up with the idea of marketing soap in individual bars and calling it Sunlight, he could not have foreseen the worldwide demand he was creating, which would lead ultimately to a huge international company, a place in the House of Lords and Port Sunlight – the village he created to house his workers. All the men pictured in this postcard from 1910 would have had homes in the village, which were initially only available to Lever employees.

This is another card in a short series of views inside Levers factory at Port Sunlight, showing the exclusively female packing room for Lux soap, another popular Lever brand. Most of these employees would have also rented houses in the village. In 1980 tenants were finally allowed to purchase their homes and all property in Port Sunlight is now available on the open market, although building restrictions are still strictly enforced by the company.

Birkenhead Docks.

Many thousands of men worked within the Wallasey and Birkenhead dock system before its gradual decline. Built in the 1830s, 110 acres of water were enclosed to form the Great Float, with the largest grain warehouses in the world lining its banks. Based on an Italian campanile, the tall building pictured was the central hydraulic tower and engine house, which supplied the power to open and close the lock gates among other functions. the tower lost its upper roof to an air-raid, but the rest of the building survives.

Scene in Lairage. BIRKENHEAD.

Due to an outbreak of disease in British cattle and sheep caused by the live importation of animals from South America, Birkenhead lairage was built in 1886 to improve the monitoring of this trade, the lairage being the only place where foreign cattle could be landed and slaughtered. Located to the south of Morpeth Dock, it had its own landing stage, pontoon bridge and rail links. Times have certainly changed from when it was acceptable to publish such a postcard.

Shop work accounted for roughly half of the workforce at the turn of the twentieth century and looking at old postcards of the period it is easy to see why. The postcard shown here is of the junction of New Chester Road and Bedford Road in Rock Ferry and shows rows of shops all the way up to Rock Ferry station. Little survives today but the bank on the right still stands. The building opposite has lost its shopfront but the white house behind is extant.

With the pressures on the High Street through online shopping and high business rates ever greater, few shops are able to withstand the onslaught. One of the limited few not susceptible to the internet are small hairdressers such as the one illustrated here, which once stood at the bottom of Prenton Road West in Birkenhead. Such places were the lifeblood of the community, but many have been converted for domestic use.

Regarding the ongoing loss of local shops and amenities, one of the few areas to buck the trend is Oxton village in Birkenhead. The row of shops shown here is in Rose Mount and all the property survives as going concerns, including restaurants, clothing outlets, general stores and a post office. Oxton was an early rural hamlet that subsequently expanded into a Victorian commuter settlement. It contains no fewer than sixty-four listed buildings and is a designated Conservation Area.

The thriving community seen here in Wallasey Village was not so lucky, with many of the local workforce having to move out of the area when most of the property shown here was demolished. The only building to survive the onslaught was the gabled row on the left, which still stands on the corner of Stonehouse Road. The white building sticking out on the right was the original Black Horse, which came down when the licence was transferred to a larger pub of the same name built further back.

Wirral's water supply originally came from boreholes that were dug to various depths throughout the peninsula, supplemented by water from the Alwen Reservoir in North Wales. Most is now taken from the River Dee via extraction plants. The old water tower illustrated still stands near Bidston Hill, but the fine chimney has been lost and the adjacent small reservoir has been filled in and used for housing. Similar structures remain at various high points of Wirral.

Storeton Quarry has been providing building stone since the Roman occupation. Its creamy sandstone has been used for Birkenhead Town Hall, Lime Street station and even cladding for the Empire State Building in New York. For the men who worked the quarry it was hard and dangerous work, with few, if any, of the modern safety measures in place. The quarry was 200 feet in places, eventually being filled in with spoil from the Queensway Tunnel in the 1930s.

Frosts Mill, Ellesmere Port.

Formerly known as Whitby Locks, Ellesmere Port grew up around the terminus of the Ellesmere Canal. Canals enabled the bulk transportation of goods such as coal, ceramics and grain. This led to the construction of large mills and warehouses at the side of the canal such as the two illustrated on this page. Frosts were a large company based in Chester who constructed this mill in 1906 after a large fire destroyed their Chester premises. The same fate befell their Ellesmere Port mill in 1970, two years after closure.

Grain Elevator, Ellesmere Port

The grain elevator pictured above was used to store grain, which arrived on the canal in bulk. It was then moved into the three mills constructed around the same time, namely Imperial Mill in 1904, Kings Mill in 1905 and Frosts Mill in 1906 for processing. The postcard also captures the corner of Shropshire Row on the left, a residential terrace for dock workers, and a distant view of Mount Manisty, which was created from the spoil from the excavation of the nearby Manchester Ship Canal.

5

Transport

Birkenhead Tram 51 of 1902 – one of the Prenton Bogies.

In 1860, Birkenhead became the first town in the country to have a tramway system. Originally horse-drawn, the system was electrified in 1901 and continued in operation until 1937 when buses took over the operation. Tram 20, illustrated here, was of 1915 vintage, its route being from Woodside Ferry where most of the routes began, via Conway Street and Park Road West to Shrewsbury Road where there was a tramway station at the top of Palm Grove.

Wallasey had to wait until 1878 to get their horse-drawn trams, with electrification following in 1902. The first three routes started at Seacombe and terminated at New Brighton: one via Rake Lane, one via Warren Drive and the most direct route along Seabank Road. The accident shown here from 1907 shows car No. 36 after it had jumped the rails and hit a garden wall. No one was hurt but the council had to pay £15 for the damage.

Trams were illuminated on so many different occasions, ranging from the annual Central Park Carnival, fundraisers for the Lifeboat Institute and royal visits – Car 54 was permanently rigged up for this purpose, continuing to light up the streets throughout the First World War and beyond. The occasion captured on this rare postcard was the visit of George V and Queen Mary on 25 March 1914 when he came to lay the foundation stone for the new Town Hall.

Although the Birkenhead tramway system was based at Woodside Ferry, a large car shed was based on Laird Street, as illustrated on this postcard from around 1910. Built in 1900–01 it eventually had room for sixty tramcars. There were also capacious workshops with a hydraulic wheel press and screw-cutting lathes, a woodwork shop and a smithy. The complex was known as the north end depot with the south end depot being located in New Ferry.

This view captures an Atlantean bus in Wellington Road, New Brighton. The rear-engined Atlanteans were introduced into the Wallasey Corporation bus fleet in 1958 – the first in Britain to do so. They were the first to have driver-only operation and had a much greater capacity, being capable of carrying seventy-seven passengers. This reduced the number of buses needed on the busier routes and the gradual phasing out of both the front-engined buses and of bus conductors.

The introduction of the Atlantean buses into the fleets of Wallasey and Birkenhead certainly made economic sense but it also led to the loss of the older front-engined Guy and Dennis buses, which many Wirral residents will remember with fondness. The No. 80 route Guy Arab bus captured here on the Prenton Circle route is heading down Prenton Hall Road towards Woodchurch Road. These buses ran from 1955 until the late 1970s. (Copyright A. Murray-Rust)

Seacombe Ferry was a large transport hub during the first half of the twentieth century when the Mersey ferry boats linked up with many of the local bus routes and the nearby Seacombe & Egremont railway station. Passenger traffic ceased at the station in 1962 and most of the bus routes no longer terminate here, even the ferry boat is an occasional visitor now and the large car park to the right in this 1970s view is now a space museum.

Woodside was also a centre for road, rail and ferry, similarly declining during the 1970s and '80s. The demolition of the large Victorian railway station was a particularly grievous loss as it was one of the grandest mainline termini outside London. The view here is from a postcard c. 1965 showing a selection of diesel Dennis buses in their fine blue livery before the MPTE decided to repaint the entire Wallasey and Birkenhead fleet in an admixture of sea-green and blue.

TSMV (twin-screw motor vessel) *Royal Iris* was known to everyone on Wirral as the fish and chip boat due to its odd yellowy livery. It entered service on the Mersey in 1951 and proved so popular that Wallasey Transport even built a road-going replica for the tourist market. The boat gave so much pleasure to so many people over the years that its current circumstances seem so sad: it sits languishing unloved and rotting on the bank of the Thames at Woolwich.

The Ferry Across the Mersey has become a bit of a cliché over the years, but for anyone who has ever experienced it the journey is often exhilarating and even a little scary in rough weather. The Leasowe ferry boat pictured here was used on the Seacombe to Liverpool service. Built in 1951, not on the Mersey as one might expect but in Devon, it operated until 1974 when it was sold to Greek owners who still operate it between the islands of the Aegean Sea.

This psychedelic-looking ferry boat started life as *The Woodchurch* in 1960, seeing stalwart service on the Wirral to Liverpool route for over forty years. In 2003 it was renamed *Snowdrop* and given the colourful livery seen here by Sir Peter Blake, the artist responsible for the cover of the seminal Beatles album *Sgt. Pepper's Lonely Hearts Club Band*. The paint job references the use of Dazzle ships and there is a small display on board elucidating their effectiveness in wartime.

The much-travelled MV *Egremont* entered service on the Mersey in 1951. With a passenger capacity of 1,200 it proved a reliable workhorse for many years despite having several safety issues regarding its design. It was retired in 1975 and sold to the Island Cruising Club in Salcombe in Devon, later it was used by a charity involved in the education and development of young people. In 2018 it was moved again up to Gloucester Docks for renovation work.

Most of the piers that once thrust out into the Mersey have been dismantled, the pre-eminent example being that at New Brighton, which combined a functional landing stage with an entertainment pier for the thousands of tourists that once flocked to this popular resort. The 'modern' postcard here was taken during the 1960s when New Brighton's glitter had begun to fade and the whole area had rather gone to seed. Happily, the resort has had a bit of a renaissance over the past few years and is beginning to regain much of its lustre.

The next pier down the coast was at Egremont, the longest pier on the Mersey and at one time the headquarters for the Mersey Ferry Company. Constructed in 1827, it survived until 1946 despite having been rammed several times. Nothing much remains other than the Ferry public house and a view of the rapidly deteriorating riverscape at Liverpool.

Further upstream are the two remaining working piers on the Wirral side of the Mersey, Seacombe Ferry and Woodside Ferry being the two closest to the Pier Head in Liverpool. The postcard captures the *Iris* at Seacombe in 1903 before its gallant raid on Zeebrugge in April 1918 in conjunction with its sister boat *The Daffodil*, during which action no fewer than eleven Victoria Crosses were awarded. Both boats were duly given the epithet 'Royal' for their contributions during the war.

Woodside Ferry has a long and distinguished history dating back to the early thirteenth century when the monks of Birkenhead Priory provided a ferry service for pilgrims. Other milestones were the introduction of paddle steamers in 1822 and steamers such as the *Oxton* in 1879. In its heyday the service ferried over 30 million passengers across the river annually, but with the introduction of the Mersey Road and Rail Tunnels this figure reduced dramatically. The two remaining ferries mainly cater for tourists today.

Smaller ferries near to Woodside, Monks, Birkenhead and Tranmere were gone by 1895; *Rock Ferry* lingered on until 1939. The next downstream was *New Ferry*, which has been captured by the postcard photographer in this interesting shot of 1905. It has also managed to capture *Indefatigable*, one of the old naval cadet training vessels that were permanently anchored in the Mersey. It was on the foreshore to the south that I. K. Brunel's legendary Great Eastern was broken up for scrap.

A short flight of steps cut into the rock is all that remains of *Jobs Ferry*, the next landing downstream. Far better known was *Eastham Ferry*. Known as the 'Richmond of the North', Eastham and its ferry was a Mecca for tourists throughout the Victorian and Edwardian period, and only declined in the 1930s when passenger numbers fell. Eastham Gardens contained a hotel, rides, poirrots, fountains and even a bear pit that remains to this day (minus the bear).

THE WORLD'S FIRST HOVERCOACH
THE VICKERS VA-3 OPERATED BY BRITISH UNITED AIRWAYS ON B P FUELS AND OILS

The world's first scheduled hovercraft service was inaugurated on 20 July 1962 between Rhyl in North Wales and Leasowe in Wallasey, covering a distance of 17 miles in thirty-two minutes at an average of 33 miles per hour. The 12-ton Vickers VA3 provoked a large amount of interest but would prove to be a commercial failure as the weather on the Dee proved to be unseasonably stormy this year and many crossings had to be cancelled.

The UK's first linear park was opened as the Wirral Way in 1973 along the bed of the old West Kirby to Hooton railway line, which had been created as a branch of the Birkenhead to Chester line in 1866. Hadlow Road station serviced the village of Willaston with up to twenty-four trains travelling through each day at its height. The gradual decline in traffic led to its closure in 1962 but it now has a new lease of life as a living museum.

Birkenhead.   *Central Station.*

This postcard, one of a short series made by Wrench Ltd taken of the Mersey Railway in the early 1900s, shows the northern approach into Birkenhead Central station with the old traction depot on the right, which has been removed. Fortunately, the fine canopy to the left has survived. Most of the large expanse of sidings to the south of the station have gone, along with a large gasometer, which was a landmark here for many years.

Birkenhead.   *Hamilton Square Station.*

The next station on the line was Hamilton Square, captured here in another of Wrenches postcards of the Mersey Railway. Taken during the early Edwardian period, it portrays a fine array of railway employees in their smart uniforms on the Liverpool bound platform before renovation covered up the ornate tiling and latticework bridge. Although there were three stations on the Birkenhead side, the only Liverpool station available in the early days was at James Street where some of the old tiling has been re-exposed.

6

Education

THE VISOR.

DOCTUS IN SE SEMPER DIVITIAS HABET.

BIRKENHEAD INSTITUTE
SCHOOL MAGAZINE.

CHRISTMAS, 1933.

Birkenhead Institute in-house magazine.

SEA BANK HIGH SCHOOL, LISCARD

Seabank High School was located at the top of Dalton Road in Wallasey at its junction with Seabank Road. Opened in 1892 as Miss Earps Ladies School, it eventually moved around the corner to Penkett Road where it survived until 1940. This particular postcard was sent on Christmas Day 1907 by two teachers, Miss Gadsby and Miss Hall, to a pupil at the school, Miss Lewis of Holland Road. The building is now two private residences.

This old postcard captures the original Poulton Road School, which lay between Park Road and Northbrook Road in Seacombe, Wallasey. Unfortunately, this fine building was destroyed during the Second World War by a German bomb. A new school was built after the war and has recently been rebuilt as Somerville Primary School.

Wallasey High School for Girls was situated in Mount Pleasant Road and was located at three separate sites along the road. The building illustrated here was the main block adjacent to Glen Park Road, which later became Weatherhead School before being demolished in 2004. Mount Primary School was built on the cleared site and the Weatherhead name was transferred to a site off Breck Road.

This tiny cottage was the original home of Wallasey Grammar School and served the area from its construction in 1799 until its undoubtably cramped conditions led to a move to a purpose-built building in St Georges Road in 1864. The building still stands on a grassy knoll above the busy Breck Road and is now a Grade II listed private residence. This delightful view was painted by local artist Harry Hopps who has also captured the old mill on top of The Breck.

This rare postcard illustrates the building used to house Wirral Grammar School from 1858 after its move from Breck Road. It was located in St Georges Road on a site to the north of the present St Georges Primary School when it was still called Back Lane. The postcard is one of many local views taken by Hodgsons of Cleckheaton in the Edwardian era.

Wallasey Grammar School's final move was to this location in Withins Lane in 1906 when larger premises were again required. Additional buildings of no architectural merit were built in 1963 when the site was extended into a further education facility – this has since been demolished and replaced with housing. The building pictured here now functions as Liscard Primary School.

Universal attendance for five to twelve year olds had been brought in with the 1870 Education Act, so provision was required to cater for the additional pupil numbers. Poulton Junior School in Wallasey was built for this purpose and was one of many schools constructed in Wirral to a very similar design around the turn of the last century, others being at Vaughan Road and St Georges Road Wallasey, and Woodchurch Road and Devonshire Park Birkenhead. The building closed in 2008 and was demolished to make room for housing.

One of the nearby infant schools was Park School in Love Lane, which was a feeder school for Poulton Junior School. The single-storey building seen in the background was destroyed by arson and a new school now occupies the site. The picture shows Miss Drake's class of 1964 with the author on the back row, third from the left. Most of the children captured here will be in their sixties and looking forward to retirement.

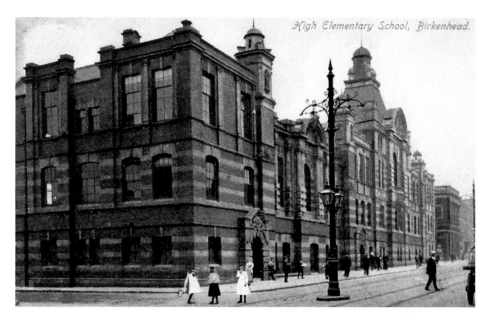

The Birkenhead Higher Elementary Technical School, to give it its full original title, is one of the grandest Edwardian buildings surviving in Wirral. It was built to house both boys and girls, each with its separate entrances which are still grandly identified in terracotta and stone. Designed by T. W. Cubbon and opened in 1905, it served the town for over eighty years, eventually being converted for use by Wirral Council as offices.

The view of this beautiful edifice was obstructed by a flyover in the 1970s, which rose up immediately in front of the baroque façade. Luckily this monstrosity was short-lived and came down in the 1990s. The whole building has now been listed as Grade II by Historic England, which should help to preserve this art nouveau treasure. All the Victorian property opposite the former school has been lost, along with the huge Ritz cinema, which closed as a picture house in 1969.

Holt Hill Convent School stood at the top of Whetstone Lane in Birkenhead where much of the original sandstone perimeter wall remains. Founded in 1852, it was run by the Sisters Faithful Companion of Jesus, a French order of nuns. It served the spiritual needs of Tranmere until 1941 when wartime bombing caused the sisters and their young charges to be dispersed away from danger to the more rural Upton Convent. They never returned, and the site was eventually sold for housing.

This school was known by most locals as Tollemache School or 'Tolley' as it stood at the top of Tollemache Road in Birkenhead, but it was also known as Birkenhead Institute, which moved here from its original site in Whetstone Lane in the 1970s. This fine neo-Georgian building was pulled down in 1994 and houses built on the site, one of the roads being named in memory of war poet and Birkenhead Institute alumnus Wilfred Owen.

Most of the land in Oxton belonged at one time to the Earl of Shrewsbury. Land was bought off the earl, a devout Catholic, by wealthy catholic businessmen to build houses such as the fine Victorian villa shown here, which was owned by the Bishop of Shrewsbury, John Carroll. He turned the ballroom in the house into a chapel and the orchard was eventually used to build a small Catholic church. Overdale was gifted to Birkenhead School in 1931 and is now used as the junior school.

KENSINGTON HOUSE, BIDSTON ROAD. (Dixon)

Kensington House School for Ladies stood at the corner of Bidston Road and Howbeck Road in Birkenhead and catered for both day pupils and boarders. The school was made up of three conjoined houses at Nos 59–61 Bidston Road and remained as such until falling numbers brought about its closure in 1934. The property survived the war but was pulled down in 1965 and a block of flats now occupies the site. Similar large properties in the area have thankfully endured.

Elliott & Fry, **ST. AIDAN'S COLLEGE, BIRKENHEAD.** London, W.

Driving along Shrewsbury Road in Birkenhead brings one to the magnificent Victorian façade of Birkenhead School. This is an all too rare survivor from a time when architecture could lift the soul. Another such building once graced the same road further north, but St Aidans Theological College, although equally beautiful, fell victim to the philistines in Wirral's 'planning' department and was needlessly torn down in 1970. A sad plaque is all that remains of this noble edifice.

Birkenhead Technical College was constructed between 1949 and 1951 and served the town for over fifty years before being demolished in 2005. The Glenda Jackson Theatre stood alongside and met the same fate, but interestingly there were persistent rumours that the theatre contained a nuclear fallout shelter. These rumours turned out to be true: it was prosaically named the Civil Defence Corps Control Centre Site 2. Built in 1952 and operational until 1968, it was reactivated in 1988, ending its life as a recording studio for the college.

Bromborough Village School in The Rake was erected in 1868 with funds provided by Mr Robert Rankin, the owner of nearby Bromborough Hall, and served the village well until its eventual closure in 1983, after which it became the local community centre, a role it continues to perform today. The old school building is adjacent to the schoolmaster's house and this group are listed as Grade II by English Heritage. Also of note is a big stone by the school wall known as a glacial erratic.

Even large schools have been lost over the years, with Rock Ferry High School being one of the biggest sites to face the wrecking ball. Opened in the 1920s as a boys' grammar school, it went comprehensive in 1968, with girls being admitted from 1980. It merged with Park High School in 2011 and the site was cleared in 2016 except for Ravenswood, a late Victorian Grade II listed villa in the centre of the site whose grounds the school was built on.

The old village of West Kirby has been rather lost in the development of the rest of the town, and the old school seems even more remote, being tucked away down a quiet lane near to the Ring o' Bells pub. This is a shame as the old building contains an interesting little museum of local history. The school building dates from 1848, closing in 1892 when it became the Charles Dawson Brown Museum. The Barton Room was built in 1968 and further extensions subsequently added.

Originally founded in 1855 by Edward Price as an extension to his prep school in Tarvin, Mostyn House School was more notably run by the Grenfell family from 1862. Wilfred Grenfell was a famous polar explorer of the 'stuff and nonsense' variety whose tales of derring-do thrilled the pupils of the school for many years. The school prospered but eventually closed in 2010 when this distinctive building was tastefully converted into flats.

Not all redundant structures meet the fate of so many recorded in this book. With a little imagination, old buildings can be put to other uses, often for the benefit of the local community. Bromborough Pool Village School was constructed in 1899 as part of the first garden suburb on Wirral, predating its far better-known neighbour Port Sunlight. The whole village has been designated as a conservation area so the school, although closed in 2006, seems safe from destruction for now.

The larger school pictured here, opened in 1910, was known as the Parade School and stands on the corner of Hoyle Road and North Parade in Hoylake. When it closed as an educational establishment, the local community fought a long and ultimately successful battle to prevent its destruction by the council. It is now used as a community centre, a most valuable local asset. How many other fine buildings could have been saved for posterity with a little more imagination and forethought?

Acknowledgements

Gratitude is due to the many, mostly unknown, postcard photographers who have captured the past for the benefit of present and future generations. They did so for commercial gain but their value as social history is incalculable.

Thanks are also due to that merry band the postcard dealers, that breed of entrepreneurs who sit behind trestle tables every weekend in draughty church halls, uncomplaining and ready to impart their knowledge.

Finally, a big thank you to all local historians and local history websites I have gleaned much information from, and to the staff at Birkenhead and Wallasey libraries.